Starting School

Carron Brown and Stef Murphy

Kane Miller
A DIVISION OF EDC PUBLISHING

Starting school
is a big deal!

There are new things to learn, great friends
to make, and lots of fun to be had!
Shine a flashlight behind the page or
hold it to the light to reveal what happens
during a typical school day. Discover
a hidden world of great surprises.

Good morning! Chloe is wide-awake and very excited. Today is special—it's the first day of school!

What's in Chloe's closet?

It's the outfit she picked
out especially for today.

Chloe can't wait
to get ready.

Ethan is dressed and having breakfast before school.

What's in his bowl?

Munch munch!

His bowl is filled with tasty
oatmeal and fresh fruit.

This breakfast is full of good energy to
keep him going throughout the morning
and to help him concentrate in class.

Zip!

Emma's backpack is ready—it's packed with everything she needs for school.

What's inside?

It's a pencil case.

Inside the case, there are pens, pencils, crayons, an eraser, and a pencil sharpener.

Other pockets of her backpack hold her lunch box and water bottle.

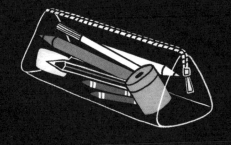

Mateo is waving goodbye to his parents.
He's a little nervous to ride the bus,
but he's not alone.

Who else
is inside?

Hi!

There are lots of other children
riding the bus to school, too.

The driver makes sure everyone has a seat.

Chloe is looking out of the window
with her new friend Mateo.

What can they see?

It's their school.

The bus is almost there.

Prisha is waiting outside her classroom.

What's behind
the door?

There are tables and chairs
for Prisha and her classmates.

The teacher has a desk
at the front of the class.

Welcome to your classroom!

The friendly teacher shows Ethan
where to hang his coat.

Where does his
bag go?

There are cubbies.

Ethan finds the one with
his name on it.

Cubbies help to keep
the classroom tidy.

It's time to get to know each other.
The teacher introduces himself and asks
everyone to say their name.

There's just one more
class member to meet.

Who is it?

It's Fred the goldfish!

Fred is the class pet. During the year,
the children will learn how to take care of him.

The teacher starts the morning with music. The children sing and play along.

What instrument is Mateo holding?

Jingle jangle!

He's shaking a tambourine!

It's fun and easy to play.

Now it's time for the first lesson.
The teacher is writing on the board.

What are the children learning?

It's math.

The children are learning about numbers and adding them together.

It's time for lunch. Emma is sitting
at a table with her new friends.

What's inside
her lunch box?

Yummy!

There's a sandwich, crunchy carrot
sticks, some raisins, a sweet,
juicy apple, and a drink.

Eating a healthy, balanced
diet makes it easier to
learn and play.

Everyone is back in the classroom, but they're sitting on the floor.

What is happening now?

Shhh!

It's story time.

The teacher is reading aloud and showing the children pictures from the book.

The bell rings—it's recess.
Recess is the time for everyone to take a break.

The playground is busy and bustling—full of children doing different things.

Where is Chloe?

Whoosh!

She's going down the slide.

It's good to run and play in the fresh air.

The last part of the day is for art.
Being creative is so much fun!

What is Prisha painting?

She's painting the sun.

Prisha will take her painting
home when it is dry.

The first day of school is over, and it's time to go home. The teacher tells each student goodbye. He is so proud of his new class!

Mateo says goodbye to Chloe.

What is he giving her?

It's a painting of the two of them.

Chloe says thank you to Mateo for his gift.

School is a great place to make friends.

At home, Chloe tells her family
all about her first day of school.

There's a lot to talk about—the bus,
her friends, her teacher, the lessons,
Fred the fish ...

She can't wait to go
to school tomorrow!

There's more...

Every school is different, and each school day has new surprises. Read more about some of the things you might see and do at school, and learn about some of the people you might meet.

Teacher

In most kindergarten and elementary school classrooms, one teacher has the same class of students for a school year. A teacher's job is to help students learn how to read, write, do math, and find out lots of different things about the world.

Principal

The principal is in charge of the whole school. It's the principal's job to make sure everyone in the school works well together. A principal often leads school assemblies, when the whole school gathers for special occasions or to hear school news.

Classroom

A classroom is where lessons take place. There may be whiteboards and computers, as well as books, posters, games, and other tools for learning. Usually there are cubbies to put away bags and coats. Some classrooms have a class pet.

Library

A library is a place where books are kept for students to use and enjoy. A classroom might have its own small library, or there might be a large library for the whole school.

Lessons

There are all kinds of lessons at school, including math, art, reading, science, and music. In math, students might learn all about numbers, shapes, counting, and telling time. Art lessons can get messy!

Cafeteria

About halfway through the day, everyone stops for lunch. Some children might bring a packed lunch from home. Other children might get their lunch from the school cafeteria.

School bus

Some children walk or cycle to school, others go in the car, and many take the bus. Bus drivers welcome children at the start of the day and drive them to school. They also drive the children home at the end of the school day.

School nurse

A school nurse helps students to stay healthy and takes care of them if they get hurt or feel sick. If anyone is unwell and needs to go home, the nurse stays with them until a parent or caregiver can pick them up.

First American Edition 2022
Kane Miller, A Division of EDC Publishing

Copyright © 2022 Quarto Publishing plc

For information contact:
Kane Miller, A Division of EDC Publishing
5402 S 122nd E Ave, Tulsa, OK 74146
www.kanemiller.com
www.myubam.com

Library of Congress Control Number: 2021937015

Printed in Shenzhen, China. PP1021

ISBN: 978-1-68464-283-0

1 2 3 4 5 6 7 8 9 10